T0123464

Journeys to Home

Janna Benson Kontz

Inspiring Voices®
A Service of Guideposts

Inspiring Voices books may be ordered through booksellers or by contacting:

Inspiring Voices
1663 Liberty Drive
Bloomington, IN 47403
www.inspiringvoices.com
1-(866) 697-5313

Because of the dynamic nature of the Internet, any web addresses or links contained in this book may have changed since publication and may no longer be valid. The views expressed in this work are solely those of the author and do not necessarily reflect the views of the publisher, and the publisher hereby disclaims any responsibility for them.

Any people depicted in stock imagery provided by Thinkstock are models, and such images are being used for illustrative purposes only.

Certain stock imagery © Thinkstock.

ISBN: 978-1-4624-0484-1 (sc)
ISBN: 978-1-4624-0483-4 (e)

Library of Congress Control Number: 2012923768

Printed in the United States of America

Inspiring Voices rev. date: 01/03/2013

Dedication

This book is dedicated to my parents, Curtis and Jacquelyn Benson, who taught me to live with grace and faith ... and to my husband, Doug, and daughters, Kori and Britta, who teach me to live with grace and faith each day.

Contents

Foreword

From the beginning of our lives to the end, the uncertainty of our transition in our final moments remains a part of our subconscious. Most of us wonder, "How do we wrap up the gift that has been our lives? What will be our final legacies? Who will help us come to terms with dying? What will come after our death?" *Journeys to Home* looks at these questions in a beautiful and satisfying way.

My first experience with Pastor Janna Kontz as a Hospice Chaplain was very personal. My beloved younger sister, Laurie, was in the final hours of her life. Janna came to her bedside to comfort her and her family as we struggled to face the inevitable. The serenity and faith Janna embodied and shared helped us immensely as we experienced my sister's transition between life and death.

In this collection of stories by Janna Kontz, we are offered a rare insight into the final days and moments of those who are at their end of life. It also reflects the emotions Janna experiences as she offers comfort to them. Told with the sensitivity, purity and simplicity of the prairie landscape, Pastor Kontz shares the fragility and the miracles in her work. From those who resist the inevitable to those who embrace it, this Hospice Chaplain cannot escape being touched and reaffirmed by those who are making their journey home. The reader is left with the sense that there is truly a master plan in our living and in our dying.

Doreen Rosevold
Author of *Farmwife Diary*

Preface

I took the job of hospice chaplain as a concession, a stopgap. Just a job until I received another call to a church. Little did I know that I would fall in love with the people I served and find my true calling. I have learned that God calls us beyond what we expect. God calls us into, perhaps, what we least expect. I never in a million years expected to love my work with hospice.

This book is a labor of love. So is my work with hospice. You see, as a chaplain, I am responsible for spiritual care for our patients. This may sound easy. I'm a pastor, after all. But I've learned that spirituality runs much deeper than religion. Religion may or may not be a part of a person's spirituality. Spirituality is part of a person's very being. It is, I believe, ingrained in our souls. Some people completely overlook their spiritual selves, which is very sad. Some people are so deeply comfortable and comforted by their spiritual selves that they can imagine no other way. I envy them. I learn from them. I long to be like them.

These chapters bear the names of people. The people and the stories are real. Some events have been combined and the names changed to protect privacy. The photos are from my own collection. I was surprised when I looked through my photos to see that many chronicle a journey in some way or another; others tell of God's creativity, of beauty in the midst of death, of paths yet untraveled. My spirit is fed through the lens of my camera.

Read these pages through the lens of your own spirituality. The dying are not to be feared but embraced. After all, we are all dying from the day we draw our first breath. Living is learning how to navigate the time in between. May these stories bless you as they have blessed me. May they change you as they have changed me. Blessings on the journey.

Janna

Lydia

LYDIA SPOKE VERY LITTLE OVER the three years I was her hospice chaplain. Mostly, she lay in bed, although some days, she was up in her wheelchair. She rarely spoke—I heard her just twice in those years. She never moved much. She rarely opened her blind eyes. She could hear only slightly with her right ear and then only when one shouted directly into that ear. This was Lydia's life.

I visited regularly, and a couple of times I saw a glimmer of life. It made me realize that maybe all those times of bellowing the Lord's Prayer into that almost-deaf right ear might have been important to Lydia.

A break in her shell came as she was fed dinner one day. The CNA fed her some pureed meat, and Lydia shouted, "That tastes like paper!" No doubt. Another time I had cranked up the volume on my MP3 speakers to earsplitting. I set the speakers by her ear, and a local musical trio sang "How Great Thou Art" in perfect harmony. When the song was over, Lydia shouted, "Sing! Sing! Sing!" We have listened to lots of music since then. At one visit, I sat with Lydia in the hallway by the nurses' station, and one of the off-duty nurses came in with a puppy. She set the puppy in Lydia's lap, and I picked up her hand to guide it to feel the downy softness of the fur. No response. Then that little wiggly tan puppy decided to take matters into his own paws. He put those paws on Lydia's chest and started to lick her face. Lydia broke into giggles.

Miracles are realized through pureed meat, inspiring music, and wet puppy tongues.

Lois

"IT'S TOO BEAUTIFUL HERE TO open my eyes."

Those are the first words I heard from Lois. Lois was a new admit, so it was my first time to meet her. I didn't know much about her, but I knew she had been basically unresponsive for at least a couple of days. Her husband was there with her. He appeared in a dress shirt and bow tie and was a little hunched over, but he had a strong handshake. I introduced myself to him first and then went to the bed. "Lois," I said, "I'm Janna, and I'm a chaplain with hospice."

That's when the words began to spill from Lois's seemingly mute self. "I'm sorry I can't open my eyes, but I don't want to. It's too beautiful. The music is beautiful. Look. Look there. I can see God's face … and hear the music. Oh, it's so wonderful." I assured Lois I was still there and laid my hand on hers. She didn't move but continued to talk about the beauty and wonder she was seeing with her closed eyes. And then she was done. The words stopped, her eyes still closed.

I looked back, and her husband was literally on the edge of his seat. His face fairly glowed as he looked at Lois with an expression I couldn't really identify at the time. I think it was a mixture of love and peace, of disbelief and belief. It was a look of faith and relief and awe. I sat with him for quite a while after that. Neither of us spoke. I don't think there was anything we could say. Finally, it was time for me to leave. "Would you like me to visit again?" I asked.

He looked at me and said, "Well, yes! You're the only one she's talked to!"

I don't know why I was chosen to hear those amazing words from that amazing lady. But I do know that we got a glimpse of heaven that day. Lois died that evening. I believe she was already in the arms of God.

Mike

MIKE WAS MY FIRST PATIENT who was younger than me. Trust me, that hits hard. There have been quite a number of them since, and each time brings me back to earth with a crash. But Mike was the first.

He was stubborn. He would adamantly say he didn't need chaplain visits and then at the end of our visit say, "When are you coming again?"

I teased him that he just wanted a warning, and he would smile and say, "Yup, that's it!" He never wanted to go very deep at first. We spent a lot of time in silence. It's what he seemed to need. The TV was always on and muted. He never looked at it. His very large yellow lab would usually crawl up on the couch beside me like a furry sentinel to our silent conversation.

One day Mike said, "I need you to talk to my kids."

Mike and his wife had five of them—two out on their own and three still at home. They were always in school when I visited. I hadn't even met them. Panic wriggled through my stomach. "You want *me* to talk to them? But Mike, I've never even seen them!"

"It's okay," he said. "They know you're okay. I've told them."

Wow. I hadn't even realized he thought I was "okay," much less recommended me to his kids. That wriggle of panic turned into a full-blown case of inadequacy.

He went on. "I've already asked the social worker. She said you could maybe work together."

Ah, that felt much better—a team to work alongside. I was no longer an island surrounded by teenagers angry at their dad's disease.

We did have a family meeting. It went as well as can be expected. But the amazing part was that after that meeting, Mike wanted regular chaplain visits. They had been rather hit and miss before. We still had our times of silence, but interspersed with them were some pretty deep and profound conversations. Once everything was out in the open with his teenagers, Mike felt much more comfortable talking about his life, his family, his faith, and what his sons' future might look like without him.

I was privileged to be holding Mike's hand in prayer when he took his last breath. His wife and five kids were right there with him, all holding hands, all praying. It was an honor to have been a part of Mike's journey from anger and self-pity, to acceptance, to him guiding his family through the rough waters of cancer and his eventual death. He taught me so much. He taught me that silence is not only golden; it is also vital and alive and precious. He taught me, through his insistence that I could do it, how to help teenagers through the illness of a parent. He taught me that *doing* isn't nearly as important as *being*.

Thanks, Mike.

Jane

"**WE'LL HAVE COOKIES IN HEAVEN.**"

Those are the last words I heard from one of the sweetest ladies who ever lived.

I knew it was my last visit to Jane. I could feel it—in the house, in her family, in my bones.

We had spent some wonderful time together. Jane was a pillar of faith but not just blind faith. She was always questioning, always studying, always growing. When I would walk in the door of her little green house, I knew a Bible study would ensue, and I relished those days. She was smart, gentle, challenging, and kind, and she always had cookies. Now, we hospice folk don't usually accept cookies or coffee or whatever is offered to us, but it wasn't to be questioned at Jane's house. When I came, her son, who was living with her and caring for her, would plop a homemade cookie and a cup of coffee in front of Jane and another in front of me, and the Bible wrangling would begin. When I first visited, Jane still baked her own cookies, but as time passed, she got too weak to make them. So her son Brad would bake them. As her disease progressed, she would eat only a few crumbs of her cookie, but she would still insist that we have them.

On that last visit, Jane was in the hospital bed in the living room. She looked small and frail. Her family was gathered. It was the only time that I refused a cookie, but I shouldn't have. Jane, even in her weakened state, was determined that I should have one. Finally, I told her that since we couldn't share cookies and coffee together today, I'd rather not. She was okay with that. We talked then. We talked about her time being very near. We talked about how great all her kids had been and how she would get to see her husband again and the baby daughter who had died at only three days old. Finally, I could see that Jane was getting too tired to visit. I sat and held her hand for a few more minutes and read her favorite verses from Romans 5, and then we prayed. It was hard for me to say that prayer that day through the lump in my throat and the tears in my voice.

I thought Jane was asleep as I said my good-byes to her family. As I reached the back door, I whispered a quiet good-bye to Jane. I turned toward the door and heard her faintly say, "Next time, we'll have cookies in heaven."

Bonnie

"**I**'VE FIRED THREE OTHER HOSPICE chaplains."

Great first words to hear from a patient! Of course, she hadn't "fired" them, but she had told them in so many words to "get lost." You see, Bonnie was a character. She was stubborn and seemed to have a very crusty exterior. Her first words left me slightly terrified, but I thought, *Well, if I'm the fourth on her list, so be it.*

So I cleaned off a chair in her cluttered home and sat down. "Tell me about it," I said, and she did. I was there for over an hour, and it seemed that some kind of invisible bond had been formed. From then on, Bonnie not only accepted my visits but also planned for them, always with some kind of challenge for me when I arrived.

Oh, she was ornery all right. She could swear like a sailor and cry like a baby in the same conversation. She loved chocolate and loved that I loved chocolate. She knew that she was dying but was committed to living every minute. More than once, I arrived for a visit to find her by the door waiting for her ride to take her to the store—not because she needed anything but because she enjoyed the shopping. We exchanged sewing patterns and ideas for new inventions. I listened as she railed about her family one minute and bragged about one of them the next. We sat together through tears of sadness and tears from laughing so hard that we couldn't contain them.

Once Bonnie realized she could trust me, she would allow me to pray with her ... sometimes; other times she would simply say, "Not today." We developed a level of mutual respect. The first time that Bonnie asked me for a hug when I was leaving, I got to my car and broke into tears, I was so touched by that small act. I was impressed by both her strength and her vulnerability.

I got to officiate at Bonnie's funeral. As always, it was an honor to preach the pure gospel. The difference was that this time it was for my cantankerous, outspoken, blunt, intelligent, and big-hearted friend. Go with God, Bonnie, go with God.

Tyler

I REMEMBER WHEN MY GIRLS WERE babies. They were so soft and so cute ... and so healthy.

Tyler isn't healthy. He is little. And he is cute: his smile will melt your heart. And he is dying. It breaks my heart. I can't even imagine—thankfully—how these parents must be feeling. What happens to you as a parent when your baby smiles and coos, and you know you cannot save his life? Do you bargain with God? Do you offer to give your own life in his stead? Do you deny reality? Do you fantasize about him growing up to be a doctor or a great orator or a scientist who cures this ugly disease? I would guess all of the above ... and more.

Tiny pink toes and wispy dark hair should not need hospice. Chubby cheeks and cutting teeth should be just the beginning ... not closing the door on a life. Why, God? ... Why?

Road Warrior

C OLD ... SOME OF THE FIRST cold weather of the fall. Today felt bone-chilling ... cold. In spite of that—or perhaps more in the face of that—I needed to drive the ninety-seven miles to Thief River Falls. It was okay. It wasn't raining or snowing. There was just this chill in the air, and of course the air was moving ... from the north ... at around thirty miles an hour.

The day went without a hitch. It wasn't late when I started for home, so it was still light. And I was more than anxious to cover that ninety-seven miles and be home ... in the warm.

Now, keep in mind that the road between St. Hilaire, Minnesota, and East Grand Forks isn't exactly a traffic jam at any time, day or night. It's a good road for sitting back and praying as you drive. And so I was sitting back, heading into the setting sun, and praying ...

All at once there was a car. It was pulled off on a side road – a four-door sedan – nothing out of the ordinary. I zoomed by. And then it registered. There was an older couple standing by that car. Just standing there! After a U-turn, I was hopping out and asking what the trouble might be. Seems they had gotten out to switch drivers and mistakenly locked their keys in their running vehicle. With both cell phones. With their coats and gloves. And there is nothing whatsoever to stop that thirty-mile-an-hour wind … on that chilly day.

That day I learned how to break into a four-door sedan. The sobering part of that was that it didn't take long! Perhaps we were driven by that cold wind or simply by the hum of that running engine. Whatever it was, we got into that car and that couple was warm again and on their way again.

Later that week, I got flowers. I could not figure who would send me flowers. You see, I had never told them my name. They asked why I was on the road and I told them that I was a hospice chaplain heading home to Mayville. This is how small communities work: they called the flower shop in Mayville and told them they were looking for a hospice chaplain—and I got flowers.

Rose

$\mathcal{A}$ CAT. THAT WAS ROSE'S DYING wish: to have a cat to snuggle and to pet and to lie with her on her narrow bed. But Rose no longer had a cat at her little farm, so this was a problem. Her children all wanted to grant her wish, but they were from far away and couldn't bring their own cats to visit. I knew my cat just wasn't the type to take to a stranger and expect anything other than squirming to get away and hide. I visited Rose often, and each week she would talk about having a cat.

So one week I brought her one. It was a calico ... very soft, very snuggly, very stuffed ... with a tag on the ear. I didn't know if it was the right thing to do—didn't know whether Rose would accept this offering or see it as silly. I didn't need to wait long to find out. I took the cat out of the bag (literally) and handed it to her. Rose got tears in her eyes. She took this stuffed calico gently into her arms and petted it and talked to it. She knew it wasn't real, but she also knew it was real enough. Her daughter was grateful to have a cat that didn't need care—she was stretched enough caring for Rose—and she was grateful for the comfort this brown and white and black ball of fur seemed to bring.

That cat "slept" with Rose in her bed for the rest of her days and nights. It seemed she was comforted by that stuffed animal and allowed it to become her companion and even her confidante. Rose became less demanding and more satisfied with who she had become … more accepting of her disease and how it had changed her life.

Rose was buried with "Midnight," the cat, in her casket. Silly? I don't think so. God can work even through the blotchy fur of a stuffed cat.

Lyle

"**I**'M NOT A RELIGIOUS MAN, you know." That's how Lyle would begin each of our visits. He just wanted to make sure I knew that religion was not our purpose for the day. Mostly our purpose on those visits was to get to know each other, to learn to trust each other, and eventually to develop a strong bond of friendship.

When we first met, I was sure that Lyle's first line would be followed shortly with a refusal of chaplain services. I was pretty certain I wouldn't be traveling to his house again. But at the end of that first visit, I was shocked to hear, "You can come again. Just remember … I'm not a religious man."

I did my best to remember that. As time passed, we discussed the difference between religion and relationship … how it's entirely possible to have a relationship with God without religion entering into it. Lyle liked that. He would tell me how

he believed in God. He was not well educated. He had worked hard his entire life.

At sixty-seven years of age, he had never been inside a church. In this little corner of the world, that in itself is almost unheard of. His parents never went to church but did teach their boy about God. As he grew, he never felt comfortable going into a church, so he just never did. He was very comfortable in his faith. I found him fascinating and rather refreshing. God outside organized religion? Faith outside the confines of a building? Wow. Radical.

I was privileged to speak at Lyle's funeral. I got to talk about God's grace active in Lyle's life—a life lived without the circle of religion … a life lived within the circle of faith.

Connie

*E*YES THAT DANCED ... THAT WAS what I came to expect eventually. Connie looked at me with suspicion at first. Or she wouldn't look at me at all.

Connie was different than most of my patients. She lived in a group home. She had lived in various homes all her life. Connie had some developmental delays that made her life different than most of our lives. She couldn't care for herself. She couldn't talk. She had quit talking a few years back when her best friend, Donna, had been moved to another group home. When Donna was brought back, Connie never started talking again. But she could communicate. Definitely. She communicated by the look in her eyes or by turning away or—finally—with the most wonderful smile imaginable.

It took a few visits before I was graced with that smile. Connie had to learn to trust me. I took it slowly. I didn't push her or touch her at first. I would just sit. And if *The Price Is Right* wasn't on, I would talk or read to her.

Then I learned that Connie loved music. I brought my MP3, and I played some hymns. She remained unimpressed. I looked through my play list and noticed the camp songs. I started the first song, and Connie's face transformed into a witness of true delight. The second song started—"Hip Holy Jesus"—and she was rocking, literally rocking and smiling and reaching for my hand. It was a transformation before my very eyes.

On my next visit, I was greeted with a smile that involved Connie's whole body. She remembered. Connie reached for my head as I came close to her and pulled my forehead up to her own. It brought tears to my eyes. I was now a friend.

Connie left this life with the song "Awesome God" playing in her room. Connie knew an awesome God, and God's light shone through her to anyone who took the time to see it. I'm glad I took the time. I'm glad I was given the time and the patience. It was so worth it.

Road Warrior

ON THESE ROADS I SEE ... sandhill cranes and whitetail deer ... bald eagles and red fox ... coyote and Canada geese ... redtail hawks and jackrabbits ... green headed mallards and blue-winged teal ...

I drive through areas where, at any given moment, I can see more deer stands than houses.

I drive through towns where kids are on their bikes with towels flying behind them as they pedal to the pool ... or bats and gloves balanced on bikes as they ride to practice ... or they just ride the streets and sidewalks of the tiny towns because they can.

Wheat ... barley ... sunflowers ... flax ... canola ... sugar beets ... edible beans ... soy beans ... miles and miles of corn ... alfalfa ... farm girls notice the crops and give a crop report to any patient who might want it!

And some of the most beautiful clouds, rainbows, lightning, sunrises, and sunsets in the world.

Jack

H E TOLD ME ABOUT HORRORS I'd never heard or thought of. He told me about a faraway place with faraway names and faraway stories. He told me about being rejected by his own hometown. He told me he thought he was going to hell for what he had done in Vietnam. He told me of a guilt he had carried for forty years that wouldn't let go of him. He told me of pain much deeper than the shrapnel that had pierced his thigh or the cancer that ravaged his lungs.

His voice held little emotion. His expression was flat and far away. He was a man broken by a war that never should have been, part of a generation scorned for being dragged into that war in that place at that time.

I tried to give absolution. It's impossible to absolve someone who lives life in the shadow of killing children because of being ordered to do so. It's impossible to absolve someone with eyes that are empty and void. It's impossible to absolve someone who doesn't want absolution. He holds on to that time and the things he did because it's all he has left to grasp. It's not a lifeline; it's a deathline, and death will be a welcome release from the images that stomp through his waking and his sleeping.

I believe healing came only when he faced God on holy ground … holy ground flooded wholly with grace.

Olga

OLGA RARELY MOVES. OFTEN WHEN I visit, she is lying under a blanket with Psalm 23 woven into it. One day as I sat with her, I wrote this ...

The Lord is my shepherd.

Olga sleeps soundly.

I shall not want.

Her soft snores soothe the air.

He makes me lie down in green pastures.

Her tiny body curls into a C under the blanket.

He leads me beside still waters.

Peace and quiet.

He restores my soul.

Restful sleep.

He leads me in paths of righteousness for His name's sake.

Peaceful sleep.

Even though I walk through the valley of the shadow of death

No worries.

I will fear no evil.

No nightmares plague.

For You are with me.

Held in God's hand.

Your rod and your staff they comfort me.

Safe.

You prepare a table before me in the presence of my enemies.

Sound.

You anoint my head with oil.

Sweet, sweet sleep.

My cup runs over.

No hunger or thirst.

Surely goodness and mercy will follow me all the days of my life.

Deep abiding faith.

And I will dwell in the house of the Lord forever.

Dreams. Sweet dreams.

Monica

ONICA WAS GIVING ALL HER things away. And believe me, that was no small task. Unlike some homes, Monica's wasn't packed to the rafters with everything from Tupperware to tea towels. No, it wasn't like that. But Monica certainly knew a thing or two about collecting and collectibles. She had collected things all her life ... bears and dishes, T-shirts and coins. All her collections were well organized and catalogued. Everything had its place, and certain things held a place of honor.

But now she was giving all of it away—all of it! Not just a bear here and there to a friend. Not just a small stack of coins to one of her favorite school kids. No. As special as all these things were to her, she was unloading it—and in the process, unloading her life.

Monica didn't have much family. She was estranged from her

sons and her ex-husband. Her mother was still living but in a retirement community many states away. Her father and her only brother had died of the same devastating disease she now faced. So Monica knew. She knew what her future held. And she knew it wouldn't be long. So she spent her days planning. Not planning a future for herself, mind you, but planning who should receive all her special things.

When I first met Monica, I thought that her making lists and packing boxes and calling people to come to her little apartment and pick things up was a little morbid. But as we got to know each other, I realized that she wasn't morbid at all. Monica was practical. She knew she was dying. She wasn't particularly upset about that. And she wanted her collections to go to people who would enjoy them as much as she had in life. So she sorted. And she packed. She cleaned. And she remembered. As I helped her with some of the sorting and packing, Monica shared stories of who this bear had come from or when she had found this rare coin. In the midst of those stories, she shared stories of love and of pain, stories through laughter and tears.

All because she was giving her things away.

Doris

"**I** KNOW WHERE MY GIRLS ARE.**" She says it with tears. She says it with certainty. Then she tells me the rest of the story. One daughter died at the age of twenty-five. Her kidneys failed; to this day, no one knows why. "Kidneys shouldn't fail at twenty-five." She says it with tears. She says it with certainty.

The second daughter died at forty-seven—cancer. "It should have been me," she says. "I'm old. Why am I still here? I'm old." She says it with tears. She says it with certainty. And so we talk. We talk about heaven. We talk about reunions. We talk with tears. We talk with certainty.

Road Warrior

SOMETIMES THE FATIGUE OF THE day settles right into my bones as I drive home. Often that drive is well over a hundred miles. My drive home is reflection time. It is time to renew for the activities of the evening. It is time to pray—for my family, for my patients, for their families.

The stress and cares of the day can drift away ... or settle into my bones and my heart. There are days when my heart feels heavy when I arrive home. You may be surprised to learn that it's not from the grief or the constant dealing with end-of-life issues. When my heart is heavy, it is usually because family members are in conflict or not accepting of a person's disease. My heart gets heavy when our patients are children. Children should not need hospice services. I get bogged down when members of our team aren't getting along. My job makes me tired when a person denies the existence of a creator. And so I drive. I rarely get sleepy, but I do get tired ... bone tired ... dog tired ...

Then there are the days when my drive home is energizing. Light floods into my heart as I think back on a revelation reached. My spirit is light when I know deep down that I helped make someone's journey a little easier, a little more peace-filled. I can smile when I have been able to help a child come to terms with the approaching death of a parent or grandparent.

Of course this *call* is difficult. Is there anything worth its weight that isn't at least somewhat difficult? Nine days out of ten, the rewards received from working with dying patients far outweigh the difficulties. I learn so much from these people. They have changed me ... for the better.

Fern

S HE NEVER WORRIED ABOUT HERSELF. Even on the days when she could barely draw a breath through her ravaged lungs, she would ask questions about my life: How were the kids? How was our house project going? What antics did I have to share about my cat? It always amazed me that she didn't worry about herself.

One day when I arrived, Fern was sitting alone in her room. This was unusual. She was usually surrounded by people. They were drawn to her because she truly cared about them. Today she was alone. And she looked sad.

As I came in, she invited me to sit. She smiled, but it wasn't her usual smile. "The other lady who sat at my dinner table died last night." My heart ached for her. She lived in the nursing home, and she had now lost all three of her table mates in less than two months. She seemed listless. "Why am I still alive when everyone around me is dying? What good am I anyway?" I hardly knew what to say. This was not the Fern I had come to know.

We sat quietly for a while. I didn't want to give her some quick answer. Finally I said, "Fern, who is on your prayer list right now?" She picked her list out of the little cloth tote on her walker. She read off name after name—family members, friends, people she hardly knew. I said, "Did you pray for them today?"

"Well, of course I did."

We sat in silence again for a while. "Do you think they needed those prayers?" I asked.

"Well, of course they did." A smile broke across her face.

"I think God still needs you here, don't you? For today anyway?" I asked.

"I guess he does … I guess he does."

Fern was welcomed home to heaven two weeks later. She died with her prayer list by her pillow.

Ethel

S HE'S HAD A LIFE

A life filled with joy and pain

Pain that is much deeper and wider than what's physical

Grief … heartache … grief … injustice … grief

And yet there are no tears

There should be tears

So much grief deserves tears

She says she has held them so long

They no longer exist … tears …

She says she has always had to be strong

For herself … for others …

There should be tears

So much grief deserves tears

She says tears are for the weak

Why? ... Why?

Sometimes faith demands tears

Jesus wept. He grieved. He was strong.

There should be tears

So much grief deserves tears

One day the tears break forth

Like a cleansing flood they come

She weeps ... for herself ... for others

There should be tears

So much grief deserves tears

Cleansing tears ... strong tears ... faith-filled tears

Empty ... purged ... renewed ...

She says she feels like a baby ... a newborn ...

Fresh ... new ... washed ... redeemed.

Redeemed.

Ole

"**I**'M A HUNDRED AND FIVE years old, you know!" He's not ... really, he's not. But he is a hundred, so it's perfectly fine for him to think he's 105.

His age is about the only thing he forgets. He tells me the story of when he came to this country from Sweden. He was three years old then, and his mother lost him on the train. All he remembers of that is the terror that seized him as he sat alone on the platform—too scared to cry, unable to speak the language. He remembers the sheer aloneness.

Ole is sad that he cannot remember anything about his beloved Sweden. He is sad that he never got to travel back there. But then a grin breaks over his hundred-year-old face as he tells me about all the mischief he and his older brother used to initiate with the other kids at school. He winks as he says, "Sometimes I think my mother wished she had left me at that station!"

His face goes serious again as he talks about his mother and the faith that brought her to this country to join his father. A tear runs down the grizzled old cheek as he recalls his father's death. He fell out of the hay mow when Ole was only ten. Again, he remembers his mother's strong faith and how she and her young boys worked from sunup until sundown just to keep the farm running and feed themselves. A sad smile tugs at his mouth when he tells me about his Sadie and how she has been gone now for more than thirty years. His eyes twinkle when he says, "It won't be long now. I'll get to see her beautiful face again."

Ole's faith runs as deep as that twinkle in his eyes. His voice is weaker than it used to be, but still he sings, "How Great Thou Art" in a bass voice that's only a little shaky. He is so small as he sits in his wheelchair in his plaid pajama pants with a little bit of this morning's breakfast painting his T-shirt. He is small … but when I look at him, I see strength.

I see a strong man with muscles bulging as he throws a hay bale over the fence. I see a faithful man holding his wife's hand as she crosses over to the next life. I see a loving father gathering his brood of six for their nightly devotion and prayer. I see a man who has known the joys and sorrows of an entire century. I look at Ole, and I see faith in its purest form: faith that he will be home soon; faith that longs for that homegoing.

No One Brings a Hotdish When the Cat Dies

YES, IT'S A STRANGE TITLE for the last chapter of this book. But it is indeed true. Both our family pets have had to be euthanized since I started my work with hospice. Our seventeen-year-old all-black cat K. C. was diagnosed with cancer, and we were blessed to have about four months to spoil her (more than usual) and say good-bye.

Our eight-year-old black and white cat, Moco, was diagnosed with diabetes a few months after K. C.'s death. My own personal theory is that Moco's grief contributed a great deal to her illness. Yes, grief. We could tell that Moco was grieving. I swear to you, she would look at us with tears in her eyes seeming to ask, "Where is she?" Moco had never known life without K. C. We had eight months to say good-bye to Moco before we knew for sure that her diabetes was not to be controlled, and we had to have her euthanized as well.

Am I trying to trivialize the lives and deaths of our family members by telling the story of our cats? Just the opposite, actually. Those of you who have never taken an animal into your family and your heart will not understand this, but they become part of our families … they do. I say that our cats helped raise our daughters.

So how do we grieve for those pets? We're expected to just "get over it" and move on. Maybe someone will suggest (meaning well) that we just get another pet right away. I'm here to tell you that it doesn't work like that with people, and it doesn't work like that with our animals. Others don't understand our need to grieve over our pets, but then I'm not sure we understand that need ourselves. Perhaps we, too, think we should just "move on." We need to allow ourselves the time and the heart to grieve for these pets as they deserve … and as we deserve. It's okay.

K. C. and Moco, you made our lives so much richer in so many ways. To honor that, we remember your lives and mourn your deaths. But we've learned no one brings a hotdish when the cat dies.

Afterword

I was told when I took the call to Hospice of the Red River Valley that this was "just a job." It was one of my well-meaning pastor friends who told me this, and I was really okay with that. I had been in my first parish call for three years and in my most recent parish for eight and a half years. *Maybe,* I thought, *I can handle "just a job" for a while.*

As you can tell by these stories, this is more than a job to me. The people in these pages have not only taught me about how to die a grace-filled death but also how to live a grace-filled life. Of course there are hundreds more stories. These are the ones that have touched me the deepest and changed me the most, at least up to this point. I expect there will be more tomorrow or the next day, by God's grace.

Special Thanks

Thank you to Hospice of the Red River Valley for giving me the opportunity to work with these patients daily. Thank you to Sandi Kemmer, Carla Gauwitz, and Terry Kemmer for proofreading and editing. Thank you to Sara Lovro for editing my photos. Thank you to Inspiring Voices for getting these stories to you, the readers. Mostly, thanks be to God for God's grace active in the lives of people—maybe especially those who don't even know it.